THE EXTENSION OF FAVOR

Selina Edwards

THE EXTENSION OF FAVOR. Copyright @ 2025. Selina Edwards. All rights reserved.

No part of this publication may be reproduced, stored in a retrieval system or transmitted in any form or by any means, electronic, mechanical, photocopying, recording or otherwise without the prior written permission of the author.

Published by:

ISBN: 978-1-965635-20-9 (Paperback)
       978-1-965635-21-6 (hardback)

ACKNOWLEDGMENTS

To each of my ancestors who believed in the word of God, thank you for your relationship with God; for planting good seeds that caused your belief in Him to go forth and be seen by our Creator. Generational favor is evidence of you.

TABLE OF CONTENTS

Acknowledgments iii
Prologue 7
Chapter 1: God's Favor Amongst Generations 11
Chapter 2: God's Favor Prepares 17
Chapter 3: God's Favor Exchange for Humility 21
Chapter 4: God's Favor Grants Perfect Provisions 25
Chapter 5: God's Favor Covers 29
Chapter 6: God's Favor in His Fullness 33
Chapter 7: God's Favor Has the Last Say 39
Chapter 8: God's Favor Positions 43
Chapter 9: God's Favor of Time 49
Chapter 10: God's Favor Transforms Hearts 55
Chapter 11: God's Favor Provides Escape 61
Chapter 12: God's Favor That's Personal 67
Supportive Bible Verses 71
Special Thanks 79

PROLOGUE

Extension of Favor displays evidence of direct alignment to God's word though my personal collection of short stories. There is a direct correlation to how you live your life that impacts the favor of God over your life which also produces generational blessings.

God's favor is often overlooked because we minimize the fullness of God and His involvement in every aspect of our lives. His favor will give you jobs, homes, cars, influences and a lifestyle outside your reach for His glory.

Our heavenly Father's favor creates situations and circumstances beyond man's ability and understanding. God's favor produces what our carnal vision cannot see and what's difficult to explain. These situations and circumstances are often referred to as, "But God Testimonies."

And yes, "God allows His sun to rise on the evil and the good and sends rain on the righteous and the unrighteous" Matthew 5:45. However, "Know therefore that the Lord your God is God, He is the faithful God, keeping his covenant of love to a thousand generations of those who love him and keep his commands." Deu 7:9 NIV

Extension – an act or instance of extending, lengthening, *stretching out* or enlarging the scope of something.

Favor (N) Bible Dictionaries – Baker's Evangelical Dictionary of Biblical Theology
"Favor is the grace of God in our lives. The Old Testament often uses favor and grace interchangeably. The definition of grace is the unmerited favor of God."
Favor – "God giving us the ability to do something
which is humanly impossible for us to do."
Oxford Definitions – "An act of kindness beyond what is due or usual."
"Acceptance, goodwill, *gaining approval or
special benefits or blessings* and preferential treatment.

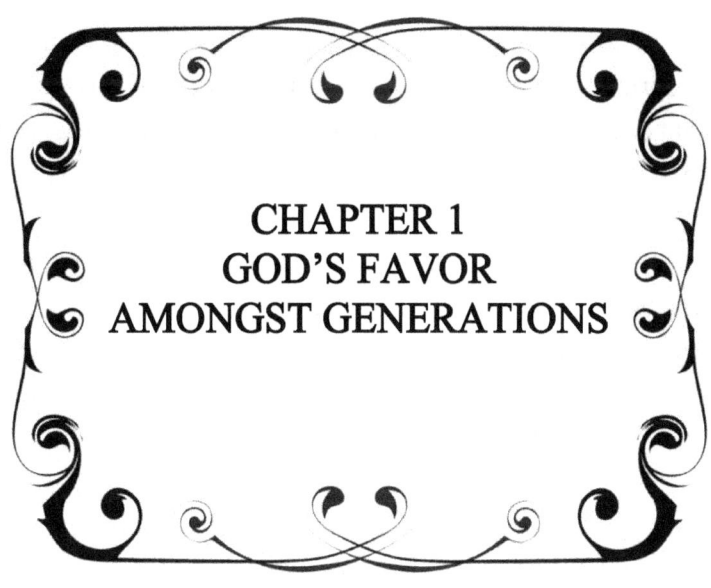

CHAPTER 1
GOD'S FAVOR AMONGST GENERATIONS

Attending church on Sundays in my family was required, it was *not* an option. There was no discussion, no debate and no compromise. I attended the same church where my father was baptized as a young adult, as well as myself, and where my daughter was christened.

It was not until later in life that I would form a personal relationship with God and start to see and understand an indescribable measure of God's favor working through me, (what was being produced) and in me (what was being transformed and developed in His image.)

Please keep in mind that God does not display respecter of persons. Romans 2:11 "For there is no respect of persons with God". However, the seed one plants will either produce a harvest that will grow and have good return, or it won't produce a righteous harvest pleasing until God. Matthew 7:16 NIV "By their fruit you will recognize them. Do people pick grapes from thornbushes or figs from thistles?"

Your obedience and relationship with God will impact your *extension of favor*. You are obedient to God's word because you believe in Him, and because you believe in Him, you reverence Him. Because you reverence Him, you love Him and because you love Him, you obey Him. Isaiah 1:19 NIV "If you are willing and obedient, you will eat the good things of the land."

David's relationship with God gave him favor to do what others would not take on and allowed him to win a battle that spectators would have betted on the other guy. My father, also named David, had an unwavering favor in his life, as well. He was born a man of color during the Great Depression in 1930. At a young age, his father left home, and he was raised by his mother, a strong, God-fearing women who did not spare the rod nor the word of God. James 5:16 "The prayer of a righteous man is powerful and effective."

When my grandfather left my grandmother with four kids, my grandmother's father stepped in and purchased her a home to raise her children. Not only did he purchase a home for my grandmother, but he did so for his other daughter, as well. My great-grandfather was a sharecropper, born in 1867.

Someone may think that my great-grandfather was just lucky or was just a hard worker. Those things matter; however, just being lucky or a hard worker does not mean that one day your luck is going to run out or that your hard work is always going to pay off. However, God's favor is undeniable, and God's favor can do what man is unable to.

My great-grandfather provided a foundation for his daughters to build on, and my grandmother passed it forward to her four children by installing godly principles. Deu 7:9 NIV "Know therefore that the Lord your God is God; he is

The Extension of Favor

the faithful God, keeping his covenant of love to a thousand generations of those who love him and keep his commands".

My father received a scholarship to play football; however, God's favor ordered my father's steps to enlist in the service. He was selected from a group of men for the Air Force while others were placed in other branches. He served in the Korean War in Japan. Once my father was out of the military, he secured a job at the Post Office. His skills got him the job, but God's favor placed him in the Special Delivery area. At the time my father was hired, he knew nothing about the Special Delivery Department within the Post Office. An opening became available, and he was transferred into the job. My father shared with me that the men within his office did not understand how my father got the job because he was recently hired and there were others with tenure that applied for the position. God's favor! My father worked thirty-eight years within the division before retiring.

When my father decided to purchase a home in a newly developed neighborhood for blacks, there were only three homes remaining. He selected one of the three homes and lived there for 60 years where he raised his four children with my mother.

My father passed away peacefully in the same home that God blessed him to secure. The same home was passed down to his daughter, and she will eventually pass it on to her daughter. "Praise the Lord! "[24] But since my servant

Caleb has a different spirit and has remained loyal to me, I will bring him into the land where he has gone, and *his descendants will inherit it*." Numbers 14:24 CSB.

My father, as a Special Delivery Person for the U.S. Postal Service, moved around town weekly and was known by many. Once my brothers and I turned working age, my father, because of his character, was able to secure my siblings and I jobs at various establishments. The same was true for myself and my daughter, as she became working age. She was able to obtain employment through the favor of her mother's character. "I was young and now I am old yet have never seen the righteous forsaken or their children begging bread." Psalm 37:25 NIV.

The same is true for parents that do not live a righteous life. Fathers and mothers that are not mindful of their lifestyles' impact their children and often their children's children until the cycle is stopped. This can be seen in households where the word of God is not present or is present but not practiced which may result in mismanagement of money, abusive relationships, poor selections of friends, negative habits, unhealthy views and so on.

Keep in mind, many of the individuals God used in the bible had some type of character flaw. They were those who attempted to commit murder, those that did murder, those that committed adultery, and the list goes on. However, their belief in God and determination to serve God was greater

The Extension of Favor

than their flaws. Their obedience was greater than their sacrifice.

We will never be flawless, and God is not looking for us to be however, God is looking for us to be consciously mindful of our daily thoughts and actions. "Those who walk righteously and speak what is right, who reject gain from extortion and keep their hands from accepting bribes, who stop their ears against plots of murder and shut their eyes against contemplating evil, they are the ones who will dwell on the heights, whose refuge will be the mountain fortress. Their bread will be supplied, and water will not fail them." Isaiah 33:15-16 NIV. Amen.

CHAPTER 2
GOD'S FAVOR PREPARES

When I look back over my life, I now understand where God's favor stepped in and covered me. He covered me when I moved to Washington, DC at the age of seventeen and kept me from many seen and unseen dangers. "If it had not been for the Lord on my side" Psalm 124 1.a.

His favor allowed me to get a job in banking two weeks after relocating to the Washington DC area which led into a 30-year career. His favor went ahead of me to install in me what was needed for my journey. In high school, I did exceptionally well in my business class where I mastered typing and shorthand. I didn't know at the time, but God was equipping me for my future. God even positioned people to be where they were needed at the perfect place and time.

Living in DC at the age of 17, away from my parents, I was free to do whatever because they could not see me, but God could and thank God that He did.

For my 21st birthday, my girlfriends invited me to a bar and suggested that I order a Long Island Iced Tea. I didn't drink; therefore, I had no idea of the contents. The alcohol in the drink was masked by its sweetness, so I thought it was harmless.

Shortly after consuming a portion, I felt nauseous; headed to the lady's room where I regurgitated the contents of my stomach. Not only was I unable to maintain my liquor that evening, but I was also unable to do so on other occasions as well. Little did I know that God was covering me. Hallelujah! Alcoholism is a disease that haunts my family.

God created me before I was in my mother's womb so that I could not consume alcohol. I had no idea of the unrevealed assignments at the age of 21, but God knew the plans for me. "Surely, Lord, you bless the righteous; you surround them with your favor as with a shield." Psalm 5:12 NIV.

Later in life, I became the matriarch of my family and was the care provider for three of my family members until God called my father, mother and brother home. Although, I didn't know what laid ahead in my future, God knew when I was twenty-one the journey placed ahead of me.

His favor kept me of sound mind while caring for my father and brother simultaneously as well as when I watched my dear mother depart from this earthly realm. God's favor was revealed while maintaining not one estate but two. God placed kind and patient strangers in my path to walk me through the estate process that went above and beyond to ensure deadlines were met and paperwork was filled out correctly. "God opens doors that no man can shut, and He shuts doors that no man can open." Revelation 3:7 NIV.

CHAPTER 3
GOD'S FAVOR EXCHANGE FOR HUMILITY

God blessed me to become an entrepreneur. We will talk more about this in a later chapter. In my thirteen years of business, I began to feel weary. The business was extremely labor-intensive. As life goes, I was aging. So, I made the decision to severely reduce the hours at my business and decided to look for employment in a less demanding occupation to supplement my income.

I recall the prayer made unto the Lord, asking Him for employment that would utilize my skills and talents to be of service. And most importantly, I asked that He place me in a work environment where I could freely express my relationship with Him.

God always goes ahead of us to make a way. In a previous role as a Program Coordinator for a non-profit, I worked with a temporary agency to assist women with job placement. I heard the Holy Spirit tell me to call my contact at the agency to let them know that I was seeking employment. Working with a temporary agency would allow me to test the waters from being out of the workforce for close to two decades. However, little did I know at the time, God was actually testing me to see if I would trust Him.

The first place the agency sent me was for an administrative position. Not a problem, as a prior project manager, I had established the skills suitable for performing in an administrative capacity. I thought, great. God, you answered my prayer and placed me in an area where my skills and talents can be applied to be of service.

The first few days on the job went well. On the third day, a woman came over to my desk and said to me "What are you doing here? You work here as an admin?" I was a little startled when I looked up from my desk, to discover that it was a client from my prior business. By the end of the day, I realized that other clients worked within the same building, and the word quickly circulated that I was working there as a temp in an admin position.

I thought I was comfortable with the job until I considered how others viewed me. I pondered over calling the agency to request a relocation, until the Holy Spirit revealed that God answered my prayer and placed me in the job. Therefore, I knew I had to honor God by staying.

Due to my prior background in leadership for over three decades, the Holy Spirit throughout my new season had to repeatedly convict me to silence my mouth, actions, and thoughts. He let me know it was ok not to be seen as the person capable of doing more or being more. It was only essential to be who God desired.

A few months passed, I started to settle into the job, and the feeling of me wanting to hide from my prior clients faded. The same women that were my clients at my business became my direct teammates. I realized the reason they were such great customers is because we shared the same love for

The Extension of Favor

Christ, and the love for Him was displayed in the work environment as well.

Things continue to get better. Into my third month on the job, I was offered a permanent position and a few months thereafter, was promoted. God did above and beyond. "For I know the plans I have for you," declares the Lord, "plans to prosper you and not to harm you, plans to give you hope and a future." Jeremiah 29:11 NIV.

Because of pride, I initially wanted to reach out to the agency and request to be placed on another assignment. However, my humility was exchanged for God's favor. "Therefore, humble yourselves under the mighty hand of God, that He may exalt you at the proper time." 1 Peter 5:6 NIV. Amen.

CHAPTER 4
GOD'S FAVOR GRANTS PERFECT PROVISIONS

A former manager shared with me that a position was opening tailored for me and asked me to apply for the job, of which I did. However, in the midst of the discussion with my manager, new circumstances arose that redirected the management team to consider someone else for the position.

Feeling betrayed, I was not going down without a fight, so I applied for the job anyway. However, the other candidate was hired. I was hurt and upset. How could management create a job for me and give the position to someone else after asking me to apply?

During the course of this period, one of my brothers fell ill. He was diagnosed with cancer and given a short time to live. The next six months became demanding as I was the care provider for my 87-year-old dad and now my brother. I attended and coordinated all my brother's and father's doctor appointments. My brother eventually moved in with me and required extensive care until his passing.

The person that was hired for the job came aboard and worked with me to create a conclusive team. She was my perfect provision. After the passing of one brother, my father passed two years later, and another brother passed three months after my father.

I probably would have lost my job, my mind, my health or all of the above if it had not been for my perfect provision. Due to her, I was able to manage my schedule to balance work and home. God's favor! He knows what we are in need of before we do.

"Therefore, do not be like them. For your Father knows the things you have need of before you ask Him." Matthew 6:8 NIV.

CHAPTER 5
GOD'S FAVOR COVERS

Prior years, I moved into a new home and was planning to close within a few months. It was only a few blocks from my daughter's new school where she was enrolled in an International Baccalaureate Program. Things were going well, and then in a matter of one day, I became part of history's 2008 recession when 2.6 million people lost their jobs. For the first time since the age of seventeen, I was unemployed. A single mother raising a thirteen-year-old.

My daughter had settled into her new school as well as the new house. She picked out the color for her bedroom walls and added her artwork to personalize the space. I did not have the heart to tell her that I had lost my job and secondly, we had to move.

If I decided to close on the mortgage, I would deplete my accumulative savings plus my severance package; the risk was too great not knowing how the recession may impact regaining employment.

An acquaintance during conversation shared how awful she felt learning that so many people were out of work due to the fall of the banking industry. She was unaware that I was part of the missive layoff. After she provided her commentary, I conveyed that the group she was feeling bad about included me. At the time, I was a very private person but was compelled by the Holy Spirit to share my story with a stranger. Little did I know that God sent her to be a blessing.

She owned several homes in the area and influenced me to look at the vacant properties, of which I did. The place I selected felt like home as soon as I walked in. The room for my daughter was much larger than her current room with a bathroom of her own across the hall. It was far more than I imagined, quiet neighborhood, spacious, with a park within walking distance. She allowed me to move in based on my severance package. God's favor! My daughter and I lived in the home for over ten memorable years.

God sent a compassionate stranger in my time of need. Glory to God! Only He can do beyond our measure. God's favor stepped in and calmed my storm and told the wind and the waters to be still. Hallelujah!

Ephesians 3:20-21 KJV "Now to Him who is able to do exceedingly abundantly above all that we ask or think according to the power that works in us, to Him be glory in the church by Christ Jesus to all generations, forever and ever." Amen.

CHAPTER 6
GOD'S FAVOR IN HIS FULLNESS

A faithful twelve-year relationship was established with my CRV Honda. God provided the car at the start of my business. He knew that the car was going to be needed for the journey ahead, to haul countless clothing donations.

Donors would look at the vehicle and say, "All this is going inside there?" and I would reply "It's not the size of the space but how well the space is maximized." Often, the donors looked at the length of the car and not the depth. We also often miss the depth of God. God wants us to view things in His fullness and not in our comprehension. Mark 9:23 NIV "Jesus said unto him, if thou canst believe, all things are possible to him that believeth."

Within my last year in business, my faithful companion, (my car), began to decline. Several repairs were made to restore her; however, with three hundred plus miles, the repairs became more frequent.

My faithful companion and I shared many road trips together and traveled to numerous unfamiliar territories as we picked up apparel from widows, widowers, businesses and organizations. We were featured on the local news with *Jessica Larche, May 27, 2014, Titled, Jessica Larche Donates TV Clothes after Weight Loss.*

One day leaving work from my 9-5 job while walking with a co-worker to the employee's garage, she asked if I considered replacing my car. As we talked, we began looking at parked cars in the garage to gain insight into my interest in a replacement vehicle. My business was closing, and I was now single. Therefore, I no longer had a need for another SRV or family type car.

The next few days to follow, my co-worker and I continued the conversation, and once inside the garage we conducted a process of elimination. On one particular day, a car caught my attention. I pointed the car out to my colleague and explained why the car was of interest. A sports event was in town for three days, and during that time, the car was parked in the same area. For the next few days, we carefully observed the details of the car.

Several months passed since I discovered my car of choice. My companion, (my car), was out of commission, and I was now car-pooling with my daughter. Determined not to rush into buying another car because I trusted when the time was right to purchase, God would let me know.

A girlfriend called me one Saturday morning and told me she was coming to pick me up to go car shopping. I mentioned to her that I was fine carpooling with my daughter, and there was not a rush. I was adamant, but she was insistent. She won, so I decided to go just to get her off my back. We drove some distance to a car dealership where she purchased her last car and had a good experience.

The car dealer drove us around the lot twice. I was not receptive to buying. I told my girlfriend and the dealer that

The Extension of Favor

God would let me know when the time was right. The dealer could sense that his efforts were to no avail. Therefore, he proceeded to journey back to the building where my girlfriend's car was parked. As we were making the same turn for the third time, I heard God say, "Look again," and there to the left of the lot, tucked away, was the car make and model from the parking garage. I had not shared with my friend about the car.

I asked the car salesman to stop so I could admire the car. The first thing I checked was the price on the sticker, and the car was out of my budget range. I returned to the salesman's car to start the journey home. I told myself that God will make it happen in His time.

The salesman asked if I liked the car, and, I told him yes. However, it was out of my budget, and I was not willing to go into debt to purchase a car. He then asked that we wait a moment while he went inside the dealership. He returned to share that the dealer reduced the price of the car. He handed me a sheet of paper with the new price of the car written down and asked if the reduced price fit into my budget. Glory to God! The price was below my consideration to invest in a car. That day, I drove away with the car of my future.

Determined not to see anything, I could have missed the opportunity to witness God's favor. We drove pass the same area twice. God is telling someone to look again! He is waiting to reveal the desires of your heart. Your favor is waiting. "And to know the love of Christ, which passeth knowledge, that ye might be filled with all the fulness of God." Eph. 3:19 KJV.

CHAPTER 7
GOD'S FAVOR HAS THE LAST SAY

Her face exhibits the goodness and faithfulness of God. During the early stages of my pregnancy, the doctor informed me that I may not be able to carry my child full term because of fibroid tumors residing in the space where my unborn child needed to grow.

Months passed and I could feel her fighting, stretching and kicking for space. As the months progressed, the fight for space became more aggressive, and the demands could be felt. Pain breached my body preventing me from functioning. I was placed on bedrest for three months.

On March 23rd, two years to the date that my mother passed, I went into labor and delivered a healthy baby girl the following morning. *Hallelujah, I say praises unto your name, Lord!* Only one of her toes showed signs of the battle she experienced while in my womb.

Within a year of giving birth to my daughter, I found myself a single mother faced with raising a child on one income. Although, millions of women do it every day and many with more than one child, when you are in the midst of the storm, you think that you're the only one standing in the rain without an umbrella.

During one of my pity parties, God spoke to me and shared, "that my daughter belonged to Him, and that He could take care of her beyond anything that I was capable of doing, exceedingly and abundantly." And so, He did!

God increased me in my career so that I could take care of my daughter and myself. There were seasons when we endured lack, but not without. She had a great education, private school for four years, International Baccalaureate studies, college and went on to receive her master's degree. Glory to God! He also selected the college she attended; that's another story. You can't tell me what God can't do!

There was tremendous pain during pregnancy, pain from the divorce, and financial hardship. But God! God's favor turned the pain into useful components equipping and strengthening us for life's journey while increasing our awareness of His faithfulness.

"Surely your goodness and love will follow me all the days of my life, and I will dwell in the house of the Lord forever." Psalm 23:6 NIV.

CHAPTER 8
GOD'S FAVOR POSITIONS

A knock on the door and there stood a Caucasian woman with a pleasant face. Her smile was inviting and warm. She handed me a bag of her undesirable garment, and I provided her with a donation receipt. The Caucasian women and I shared a brief conversation, and off I went.

During my donation pickups, I always wore a white starched cotton shirt, black slacks and fashionable but comfortable footgear. Hair pulled back in a bun with small pearl earrings, knockoffs, just in case misplaced during transporting items.

A few weeks passed and my phone rang which it did frequently with clients arranging donation pickups. The voice proceeded to say, "This is Mrs.", You were at my home a few weeks ago to pick up garments." Then she asked an unexpected question, "Do you do anything else other than donation pickups?" First thought, why? However, she is an elderly person, so I decided to respond how my parents raised me, "Yes, ma'am, I do." She then said "my lady recently had surgery and would be unavailable for a few months. She proceeded to ask me if I had time to assist and would compensate weekly." She listed the tasks as well as the salary. I told her I needed a few days to consider the offer; thanked her for the opportunity.

The job offer came during the time that I was laid off from the bank and was working a job that I dread. I was contemplating leaving the job because the conditions were not reasonable. I have worked since I was twelve years old, so for me to consider leaving a job, the environment to say the least was bad.

I pulled out my budget book and began to crunch numbers. I accepted the position as a personal assistant which lasted for over two years. One of the tasks consisted of walking her dog which I looked forward to because walking is one of my hobbies. And as a bonus, her home was in a spectacular area surrounded by water. The other chores did not feel like work as well, I drove her to doctor appointments, picked up garments from the dry cleaners, food shopped, watered her plants and house sit when she was away. God's favor allowed me to earn additional income doing things that were extremely manageable; enjoyable while supporting someone in need. It was a win-win situation.

During the time I worked for Mrs. we became friends. Mrs. and I attended plays together as well as lunch and afterwards, would occasionally stop pass Nordstrom for a few hours to walk off the meal. She entrusted me to make her apparel selections, telling the Stylist that she had her own Personal Shopper.

In addition to assisting Mrs., I started a business three years prior that I was operating in a local market. My business was flourishing; an opportunity was presented to move into a brick-and-mortar building.

The Extension of Favor

The application process for the building required a character reference. I asked Mrs. if I could use her as a reference and she agreed. Little did I know God's amazing favor that reached from a childhood relationship would show up in my life, decades later. "Do not be afraid or discouraged, for the Lord will personally go ahead of you. He will be with you; He will neither fail you nor abandon you." Deuteronomy 31:8 NIV

The real estate agent called me a few days upon receiving the application and asked me how I knew Mrs., I shared that she was a friend. He mentioned that he planned to call her, which I thought was strange because I provided him with her contact information to do just that.

Around mid-week, Mrs. conveyed that she received the call from the agent and confirmed that we were friends and said nothing further. When I received the call from the agent, he told me he was surprised that I knew Mrs. He went on to share that she grew up in the same neighborhood as his father and they lived just two doors down from each other. His father and Mrs. were old childhood companions. The agent also mentioned that she was a very prominent figure and so was her family in the community where she was raised.

The application was approved! God's favor! During my grand opening, Mrs. brought me an incredible floral arrangement. We remained friends until God called her home.

I met Mrs. because God scheduled the donation pick up in His perfect timing. The perfect season. God staged my layoff and created "her lady" to be unavailable during the timeframe of the donation pickup. He postured her heart to seek me for employment; made all the conditions right for me to accept the position. God groomed our hearts to become friends in spite of age and race differences. God made the brick and mortar become available in the perfect season and sent an agent that was the son of Mrs.'s childhood friend and neighbor. Only God and His remarkable favor! "I will go before you and will level the mountains: I will break down gates of bronze and cut through bars of iron." Isaiah 45:2 NIV.

CHAPTER 9
GOD'S FAVOR OF TIME

An estimated 350,831 people passed due to Covid-19. The year 2020 was airmarked as the year of death for the world as well as for my family. Members of my family did not die of Covid. My father passed at the age of 89 from prostate cancer and my oldest brother died 3-months afterwards from a failed heart from what I believe was due to his hero passing away, our father.

My brother was not married nor my father, both divorced. I was the oldest surviving sibling and was handed the responsibility of managing their estates.

Due to the increase in deaths caused by Covid, I was not able to give my dad a proper funeral. He was a member of his church all his life, but the church did not allow funeral services to be held on site because of Covid.

I was in the midst of trying to bring some order to my father's affairs when I learned my brother had passed. My father lived in his home for 60 years, and my brother managed a 2-bedroom, 2-bathroom apartment. Tagged, I was it.

James 1:2-4 ESV "Count it all joy, my brothers, when you meet trials of various kinds, for you know that the testing of your faith produces steadfastness. And let steadfastness have its full effect, that you may be perfect and complete, lacking in nothing."

The apartment complex where my brother resided would not allow me to enter my brother's apartment without court documentation stating that I was appointed executor of his estate. His death certificate was required by the court, and it took three months to obtain because of the backlog in cases due to Covid.

In Philippians 4:6-7, God instruct us not to be anxious about anything, but I was concerned about the rent being charged at the apartment and other utilities. And I was anxious to bring closure to both my father's home as well as my brother's resident because I was mentally and emotionally drained.

The first month passed, then the second month. My brother passed in September of 2020. As I entered the month of November, my thoughts centered on the fact that the holidays would soon be approaching, and I did not want to deal with having to clean out his apartment plus deal with the courts during the holiday season.

Finally, in December, I received my brother's death certificate, and the apartment granted me access to enter his residence. I had two days to clear out everything otherwise they would add another month's rent.

I was completely stressed and tired. Even the faithful grows weary. I was playing over in my mind a strategy to conquer packing up an entire two bedroom, two bath apartment in two days and who would help. Lord how?

The Extension of Favor

That evening prior to me having to start the process of packing up the apartment, my daughter called to check-in. She mentioned the purpose of her call was to share some good news. A longtime friend of hers, who she considered a brother and I, a son, was moving into his first apartment. The young man was the age of my daughter. He attended school with her at Christ the King, and they also attended college together at Regent University. He remained in our lives throughout the years.

I did not share with my daughter anything about my brother's apartment, but I told her that I would call her back. I immediately phoned the young man, congratulated him on securing his apartment and asked if he was in need of anything. He said, yes, everything. A weight was lifted when I heard his reply. I told him that I was clearing out my brother's place over the weekend and he was welcome to come by to take whatever he needed. He was already scheduled to be off the same weekend in preparation to move. But God!

He stopped by the apartment on the following day, identified the items of interest which were most. He called friends over to help pack up the items he wanted, and I called an organization that my brother was affiliated with to arrange a time for the members to view and take what was left.

That's not all. One of the members that came over to view my brother's belongings volunteered to help move the items from my brother's place to the young man's new location.

The gentleman worked with us for the next two days like family. He was skilled at packing, moving, and loading. He was another angel sent from God. He was patient and kind.

At the end of the second day, everything was moved out and the apartment was completely clean. If in the event I had cleared the apartment prior to December, I would have missed the opportunity to share my brother's belongings with someone dear to our family and missed the chance of blessing him. As well as to witness God's favor and miraculous perfect timing.

Ecclesiastes 3:1 NIV "There is an appointed time for everything. And there is a time for every event under heaven." Amen.

CHAPTER 10
GOD'S FAVOR TRANSFORMS HEARTS

As I sat on a stool inside the brick-and-mortal building, I began to cry and asked myself what have you gotten yourself into. I needed materials, customer bags, clothing racks, a cash register, a checkout counter, etc. The list was long, and my money was short. While pondering over my options, I heard God say to call a person in which my last encounter with was not favorable.

The request from the Lord took me back to a time when I was employed by a small business operated by a husband and wife. They owned a business supply store that furnished any and everything needed to operate a retail store from grid walls, gift boxes of all sizes, mannequins, jewelry bust, stands, display counters and more.

One day while shopping for a few items for my business, which was located at the market during this time, one of the owners mentioned that they were looking for additional help. I was laid off from the bank and looking for a means to supplement my income. They were seeking assistance to help with inventory as well as with attending business buyouts.

I applied and was hired. Roughly into the third month, one of the owners told me he needed to speak with me after the end of my shift. He proceeded to tell me that he was dismissing me effective that day because money was missing. I looked to say, what does that have to do with me. I had no exposure to any monetary transactions. I explained you have the wrong person. He said sorry, I need you to get your things and leave. I was baffled. As I picked up my handbag to exit, I turned around and said, "I may be a lot of things, but I am not a thief." Once I got inside my car, I cried, and asked the Lord, what just happened?

Fast forward, back to me sitting in the shop on the stool trying to figure out how I was going to obtain what was needed for my business, and God instructed me to call them. Very seldom have I questioned God; this was one of those times. There were two other moments in my life that I questioned God but will share those "Jonah" experiences later. Not only did I question God, but I refused to call. These individuals accused me of stealing and denied me the chance to explain. Call them to be humiliated again, no, thank you! God this cannot be the solution.

Three days passed and I was beginning to become a little unraveled. A grand opening date was established, and I had not made any progress in acquiring what was needed to furnish the store. I heard the instructions again from the Lord, clear and firm, call!

"For my thoughts are not your thoughts, neither are your ways my ways, As the heavens are higher than the earth, so are my ways higher than your ways and my thoughts than your thoughts." Isaiah 55:8-9, NIV. "Who can fathom the Spirit of the Lord, or instruct as His counselor?" Isaiah 40:13, NIV.

The Extension of Favor

I asked, Lord, how do I start this conversation, "Hello this is the person you fired and accused of stealing. I am calling because God told me to...."

And as with Moses, He shared, I will give you the words to say. Exodus 4:12 NIV "Now, go; I will help you speak and will teach you what to say."

"Now go" and this time I did what He told me to do. I called. I started the conversation by saying "Hi, this is Selina; I used to work there", and the owner, said, "I owe you an apology. The person that worked for us for over 14 years was embezzling money, and we never knew. We are sorry."

I sat in awe for a moment and then mentioned that I was glad that they were able to resolve the matter. I told the owner that I had just opened a brick-and-mortar and needed supplies. She asked me to provide her with a list. She told me that she would personally deliver the items, and she went on to say that they would open a line of credit for me for as long as I was in business, of which they did.

When she arrived at the store, she not only delivered the supplies, but also stayed to share her business knowledge. She helped me establish a credit card vendor as well as connected me with Retail Alliance, a non-profit organization that supports small businesses. The company later wrote an article on my business.

The business owner became my mentor and as of today, almost two decades ago, we are still connected. I have supported her business during seasons of transition and relocation.

As I write this, it still brings tears to my eyes. To see God's favor, we must move away from a Jonah posture and move towards a posture of Samuel, to say, yes, Lord your servant is listening and then take action.

CHAPTER 11
GOD'S FAVOR PROVIDES ESCAPE

When you know it was no one else but God. The morning was quiet as I sat preparing payroll for the staff. The doors to the store were opened to start another day of selling fine women and men apparel as well as to engage in conversation with new and familiar customers.

My head was held down as I focused on the payroll figures to ensure accuracy. When I looked up, I saw a man walking on the far side of the road, and in my spirit, I heard, "That is the devil." I did not get a good look at the man, as he only appeared as a shadow, quickly walking.

I returned to complete the paperwork and moments later a man entered the store inquiring about the location of the men's clothing. I pointed to the rear of the building. As I returned to my tasks, within seconds, the man was standing behind me with a bandana over his face and a knife in his hand. He instructed me to get up and move to the back of the building.

I recalled telling him that it was not necessary for him to hurt me and told him where the money was located. However, at this time, he shoved me and insisted that I walk to the rear of the store. I begin to beg that he take the cash and please just leave.

He shoved me again, and this time it was harder. I knew that I had a better chance of survival by remaining in the front of the store. As I was weighing my options, he was doing the same because he began to drag me to the back of the store.

My shop was located amongst four other connecting businesses. The building to the right was vacant and the site to the left was a daycare. I could always hear the children through the walls, so I began to scream for help in hopes that someone would hear me and come to my aid.

As I screamed the man used more force. To deter him from taking me to the rear of the store, I held on to clothing racks and anything that I could grab to slow down the movement. I tried to stand planted and remember the push from him that literally pulled me out of my shoe.

It felt as if the tussle lasted forever, and as I drew near the backroom, my body was in pain from the struggle. My face covered in tears. My words were now sounding like a chant, repeatedly saying, "The money is in the front of the store. Please take the money and leave."

We entered the rear of the store which is sectioned off by a wall. He pushed me once again, and I landed on the floor. The impact of my head hitting the foundation sent an echo through the room. He located a phone cord which was used to tie my hands behind my back, and at this moment I started to pray. I realized he did not come to rob the store.

My cell phone was in my back pocket, and when I fell my phone flew out of my pocket onto the floor. The man kicked the phone away from me and proceeded to walk away. I sat on the floor with my hands bound, crying and praying, Lord please don't let me die. Please help me.

Moments later, I heard a voice say "Police" and within seconds, there were three Police Officers standing over me asking if I was ok. One Officer untied my hands and helped me to my feet. I recall crying uncontrollably.

I asked the Officer if someone from the daycare called them, and he said no. I was puzzled. If not the daycare, who called? The Police Officer shared that they received a call from my nephew. My nephew? My nephew, through marriage, lived in upper New York. How did he know to call the police?

God made him call. My nephew was scheduled to get married soon. His fiancé asked him to call me on several occasions to obtain information about a photographer, but he never called. The day of the attack, she literally stood with him to ensure that he called me; when he did, he overhead the commotion. He first thought that it was a tv program until he heard my voice and called the police.

At no time did my phone ring. At no time was a call placed to him, in months. During this time, I used a flip phone. My phone was in my back pocket until it fell to the floor when I was pushed down. The phone was kicked away from me. And my nephew was able to place a call to me, but the phone did not ring. The call connected, and he was able to overhear the situation. No one but God!!!

Oh, and by the way, the <u>entire staff</u> at the daycare was on a field trip. I stopped trying to figure it out because trying to make sense of it, removes the fact that God heard my prayer and granted me favor.

The Officers stopped by the store days later to check on me and revealed, the attacker was recently released from jail for a long sentence for committing rape.

Glory to God for His divine favor and protection! God stepped in and orchestrated the events. My nephew's fiancé demanded that he call me to get information needed for their wedding and literally stood over him until he placed the call. My nephew overhead the commotion; called the police. At no time did my phone ring. I had not spoken to my nephew in months. My phone was in my back pocket the entire time until it fell to the floor when I was pushed down. The phone was kicked away from me. The phone did not ring, but the call was connected. My nephew was able to overhear the situation. But God, but God! If I had a thousand tongues and never stopped praising Him, it would never be enough!

"Jesus said to him, "If you can believe, all things are possible to him who believes." Immediately the father of the child cried out and said with tears, "Lord, I believe; help my unbelief!" Mark 9:23-25 NKJV

CHAPTER 12
GOD'S FAVOR
THAT'S PERSONAL

Thank you for taking a peek into my life. Now you know why I love the Lord as I do. I truly hope that by sharing insight into my life will encourage you to see God moving in every area of your own life. He is there!

A life with God the Father, the Son and Holy Spirit is the best investment you can ever make. God's favor has residual effects of influence, righteous pleasures, endurance, grace, protection, forgiveness, healing, comfort, joy, peace, positive relationships, victories, perfect timing, abundance of resources, and provisions for yourself and your loved ones.

I leave you with Psalm 37 by King David thought to be written to his soldiers to keep their hearts right before the Lord. It summarizes obedience and favor. It's worth reading but so is every infallible word of God. Blessings.

Psalm 37:1-40 KJV
37 "Fret not thyself because of evildoers, neither be thou envious against the workers of iniquity. [2] For they shall soon be cut down like the grass, and wither as the green herb.[3] Trust in the LORD, and do good; so shalt thou dwell in the land, and verily thou shalt be fed.[4] Delight thyself also in the LORD: and he shall give thee the desires of thine heart.[5] Commit thy way unto the LORD; trust also in him; and he shall bring it to pass.[6] And he shall bring forth thy righteousness as the light, and thy judgment as the noonday.[7] Rest in the LORD AND wait patiently for him: fret not thyself because of him who prospereth in his way,

because of the man who bringeth wicked devices to pass. ⁸ Cease from anger and forsake wrath: fret not thyself in any wise to do evil. ⁹ For evildoers shall be cut off: but those that wait upon the LORD, they shall inherit the earth. ¹⁰ For yet a little while, and the wicked shall not be: yea, thou shalt diligently consider his place, and it shall not be. ¹¹ But the meek shall inherit the earth; and shall delight themselves in the abundance of peace. ¹² The wicked plotteth against the just, and gnasheth upon him with his teeth. ¹³ The LORD shall laugh at him: for he seeth that his day is coming. ¹⁴ The wicked have drawn out the sword, and have bent their bow, to cast down the poor and needy, and to slay such as be of upright conversation. ¹⁵ Their sword shall enter into their own heart, and their bows shall be broken. ¹⁶ A little that a righteous man hath is better than the riches of many wicked. ¹⁷ For the arms of the wicked shall be broken: but the LORD upholdeth the righteous. ¹⁸ The LORD knoweth the days of the upright: and their inheritance shall be forever. ¹⁹ They shall not be ashamed in the evil time: and in the days of famine they shall be satisfied. ²⁰ But the wicked shall perish, and the enemies of the LORD shall be as the fat of lambs: they shall consume; into smoke shall they consume away. ²¹ The wicked borroweth, and payeth not again: but the righteous sheweth mercy, and giveth. ²² For such as be blessed of him shall inherit the earth; and they that be cursed of him shall be cut off. ²³ The steps of a good man are ordered by the LORD: and he delighteth in his way. ²⁴ Though he fall, he shall not be utterly cast down: for the LORD upholdeth him with his hand. ²⁵ I have been young, and now am old; yet have I not seen the righteous forsaken, nor his seed begging bread. [26] He is ever merciful, and lendeth; and his seed is blessed. [27] Depart from evil, and do good, and dwell for evermore. [28] For the LORD loveth judgment, and forsaketh not his saints; they are preserved for ever: but the seed of the wicked shall be cut off. [29] The righteous shall inherit the land, and dwell therein forever. [30] The mouth of the righteous speaketh wisdom, and his tongue talketh of judgment. [31] The law of his God is in his heart; none of his steps shall slide. [32] The wicked watcheth the righteous, and seeketh to slay him. [33] The LORD will not leave him in his hand, nor condemn him when he is judged. [34] Wait on the LORD, and keep his way, and he shall exalt thee to inherit the land: when the wicked are cut off, thou shalt see it. [35] I have seen the wicked in great power and spreading himself like a green bay tree. [36] Yet he passed away, and, lo, he was not: yea, I sought him, but he could not be found. [37] Mark the perfect man and behold the upright: for the end of that man is peace. [38] But the transgressors shall be destroyed together: the end of the wicked shall be cut off. [39] But the salvation of the righteous is of the LORD: he is their strength in the time of trouble. [40] And the LORD shall help them and deliver them: he shall deliver them from the wicked, and save them, because they trust in him." Amen.

SUPPORTIVE BIBLE VERSES

PROLOGUE

Matthew 5:45 NIV
And yes, "God allows His sun to rise on the evil and the good and sends rain on the righteous and the unrighteous"

Deu 7:9 NIV
However, "Know therefore that the Lord your God is God, He is the faithful God, keeping his covenant of love to a thousand generations of those who love him and keep his commands."

CHAPTER ONE

Romans 2:11 NIV
"For there is no respect of persons with God". However, the seed one plants will either produce a harvest that will grow and have good return, or it won't produce a righteous harvest pleasing until God.

Matthew 7:16 NIV
"By their fruit you will recognize them. Do people pick grapes from thornbushes or figs from thistles?"

Isaiah 1:19 NIV
"If you are willing and obedient, you will eat the good things of the land."

James 5:16 NIV
"The prayer of a righteous man is powerful and effective."

Deu 7:9 NIV
"Know therefore that the Lord your God is God; he is the faithful God, keeping his covenant of love to a thousand generations of those who love him and keep his commands".

Numbers 14:24 CSB
"Praise the Lord! "²⁴ But since my servant Caleb has a different spirit and has remained loyal to me, I will bring him into the land where he has gone, and *his descendants will inherit it*."

Psalm 37:25 NIV
"I was young and now I am old yet have never seen the righteous forsaken or their children begging bread."

Isaiah 33:15-16 NIV
"Those who walk righteously and speak what is right, who reject gain from extortion and keep their hands from accepting bribes, who stop their ears against plots of murder and shut their eyes against contemplating evil, they are the ones who will dwell on the heights, whose refuge will be the mountain fortress. Their bread will be supplied, and water will not fail them.

CHAPTER TWO

Psalm 124 1.a.
"If it had not been for the Lord on my side"

Psalm 5:12 NIV

"Surely, Lord, you bless the righteous; you surround them with your favor as with a shield."

Revelation 3:7 NIV

"God opens doors that no man can shut, and He shuts doors that no man can open."

CHAPTER THREE

Jeremiah 29:11 NIV

"For I know the plans I have for you," declares the Lord, "plans to prosper you and not to harm you, plans to give you hope and a future."

1 Peter 5:6 NIV

"Therefore, humble yourselves under the mighty hand of God, that He may exalt you at the proper time."

CHAPTER FOUR

Matthew 6:8 NIV

"Therefore, do not be like them. For your Father knows the things you have need of before you ask Him."

CHAPTER FIVE

Ephesians 3:20-21 KJV

"Now to Him who is able to do exceedingly abundantly above all that we ask or think according to the power that works in us, to Him be glory in the church by Christ Jesus to all generations, forever and ever."

CHAPTER SIX

Mark 9:23 NIV
"Jesus said unto him, if thou canst believe, all things are possible to him that believeth."

Eph. 3:19 KJV
"And to know the love of Christ, which passeth knowledge, that ye might be filled with all the fulness of God."

CHAPTER SEVEN

Psalm 23:6 NIV
"Surely your goodness and love will follow me all the days of my life, and I will dwell in the house of the Lord forever."

CHAPTER EIGHT

Deuteronomy 31:8 NIV
"Do not be afraid or discouraged, for the Lord will personally go ahead of you. He will be with you; He will neither fail you nor abandon you."

Isaiah 45:2 NIV
"I will go before you and will level the mountains: I will break down gates of bronze and cut through bars of iron."

CHAPTER NINE

James 1:2-4 ESV
"Count it all joy, my brothers, when you meet trials of various kinds, for you know that the testing of your faith produces steadfastness. And let steadfastness have its full effect, that you may be perfect and complete, lacking in nothing."

Ecclesiastes 3:1 NIV
"There is an appointed time for everything. And there is a time for every event under heaven."

CHAPTER TEN

Isaiah 55:8-9, NIV
"For my thoughts are not your thoughts, neither are your ways my ways, As the heavens are higher than the earth, so are my ways higher than your ways and my thoughts than your thoughts."

Isaiah 40:13, NIV
"Who can fathom the Spirit of the Lord, or instruct as His counselor?"

Exodus 4:12 NIV
"Now, go; I will help you speak and will teach you what to say."

CHAPTER TWELVE

Psalm 37:1-40 KJV

SPECIAL THANKS

Mrs. Donna L. Norma, Mrs. Mijisha Butts
and Author C. Orville McLeish.
God aligned our lives for such a time as this.
Thank you for sharing your time and talent.

Unwavering appreciation to my life support
my daughter, youngest brother and son-in-law.
Thank you for being by my side
in every major shift of my life.
I love you!

And ultimate thanks and heartfelt gratitude
to God the Father, The Son, and Holy Spirit
for vision to paper. You are my everything!

www.ingramcontent.com/pod-product-compliance
Lightning Source LLC
LaVergne TN
LVHW051156080426
835508LV00021B/2658